The D[ecline] and Fall of the American Empire

Gore Vidal

Odonian Press
Berkeley, California

Additional copies of this book and others in the Real Story series are available for $5 + $2 shipping per *order* (not per book) from Odonian Press, Box 7776, Berkeley CA 94707. Please write for information on quantity discounts, or call us at 510 524 3143. Distribution to book stores and wholesalers is through Publishers Group West, Box 8843, Emeryville CA 94662, 510 658 3453 (toll-free: 800 788 3123).

Except for the preface, the essays in this book were originally published, in slightly different form, in The Nation, *which is full of great stuff like this.*

Compilation and editing: Arthur Naiman, Sandy Niemann

Inside design: Arthur Naiman   Index: Stephen Bach

Page layout: Karen Faria, Arthur Naiman

Proofreading: Karen Faria, Sandy Niemann

Cover photo: Tony Korody/Sygma

Printing: Michelle Selby, Jim Puzey / Consolidated Printers, Berkeley, California

Series editor: Arthur Naiman   Series coordinator: Susan McCallister

Odonian Press gets its name from Ursula Le Guin's wonderful novel *The Dispossessed* (though we have no connection with Ms. Le Guin or any of her publishers). The last story in her collection *The Wind's Twelve Quarters* also features the Odonians.

Odonian Press donates at least 10% (last year it was 36%) of its aftertax income to organizations working for social justice.

Vidal, Gore, 1925–
    The decline and fall of the American empire / Gore Vidal.
       p.   cm. — (Real story series)
    Includes index.
    ISBN 1-878825-00-3 : $5.00
    1. United States—Politics and government—1945-1989. 2. United States—Politics and government—1989- 3. Vidal, Gore, 1925- - -Political and social views. I. Title. II. Series.
E839.5.V53 1992
973.92—dc20   92-23825
                                                                          CIP

Printed in the United States of America   Second printing, Nov. 1992

Contents

Gore Vidal

Gore Vidal is the author of 22 novels, five plays and countless essays, articles and reviews (see page 90 for a list of them). The grandson of Thomas Pryor Gore, the populist senator from Oklahoma, he was born in 1925 at West Point, where his father was an aeronautics instructor. Vidal wrote his first novel at the age of 19 and was widely hailed as a boy genius. Many of his subsequent novels have been number-one best-sellers.

In addition to his literary career, Vidal has twice run for office. In 1960, he was a candidate for Congress in upstate New York, where he got the most votes in his district of any Democrat in half a century. Running for the US Senate in the 1982 Democratic primary in California, he received half a million votes and finished second in a field of nine.

In 1982, Vidal won an American Book Critics Circle Award for his collection of essays, *The Second American Revolution.* The Washington Post has said of him, "I can't think of another writer more certain to have exactly the right opinion on absolutely everything."

Editors' Note

We've occasionally added brief explanatory comments or footnotes in square brackets. If you don't need them, please just ignore them— other readers may find them helpful.

Preface

Four of these pieces on the theme of empire versus republic began as speeches. Two were given at the National Press Club in Washington (they did not go over awfully well, as you might guess, but C-Span viewers were more pleased than not). One was given to raise money for PEN in New York; the last was the Lowell Lecture at Harvard in April of this year. All six were published in *The Nation.*

Essentially, I am trying to put into historical perspective the state of our union and what can still be done to salvage it. Curiously, I have had rather more effect on the presidential campaign of 1992 than I had ever dared hope. During the New Hampshire primary, Jerry Brown rang me. We had not met since our last unfriendly encounter ten years earlier when I ran against him in the Democratic primary for the Senate in California.

He had just read "Time for a People's Convention." He was excited by it. Taking America back. The concept of We the People as sole legitimate sovereign. Bringing out in the open the Ownership of the country, and so on.

Brown said he would be using a lot of what I'd been writing and saying, and I gave him my blessing. Would I come to New Hampshire and help out? No thanks, I said, but I would send him notes from time to time, which I did.

The most effective was my suggestion that he find a defense plant where he could then dramatize the necessity of converting from war to peace. He found the occasion in Connecticut. The Seawolf submarine had been cancelled by Bush. Workers would be out of a job. Clinton had promised to build more Seawolves. Jerry said, No. With the same work force and technology you must build bullet trains.

I got a call at five in the morning from Pat Cadell, saying *we* had won Connecticut. Now Clinton is appropriating a lot of the Brown-Vidal rhetoric. Whether or not he has grasped the substance we shall see when he is elected. I doubt it, but who knows?

The Day the American Empire Ran Out of Gas

On September 16, 1985, when the Commerce Department announced that the United States had become a debtor nation, the American Empire died. The empire was seventy-one years old and had been in ill health since 1968. Like most modern empires, ours rested not so much on military prowess as on economic primacy.*

After the French Revolution, the world money power shifted from Paris to London. For three generations, the British maintained an old-fashioned colonial empire, as well as a modern empire based on London's primacy in the money markets. Then, in 1914, New York replaced London as the world's financial capital.

Before 1914, the United States had been a developing country, dependent on outside investment. But with the shift of the money power from Old World to New, what had been a debtor nation became a creditor nation and central motor to the world's economy.

---

* In *The Guardian* Frank Kermode wrote: "I happened to hear Vidal expound this thesis in a New York theater, to a highly ribald and incredulous, though doubtless very ignorant audience...." Since then, my thesis has been repeated by others so many times that it is now conventional wisdom.

All in all, the English were well pleased to have us take their place. They were too few in number for so big a task. As early as the turn of the century, they were eager for us not only to help them out financially but to continue, in their behalf, the destiny of the Anglo-Saxon race: to bear with courage the white man's burden, as Rudyard Kipling not so tactfully put it.

Were we not—English and Americans—all Anglo-Saxons, united by common blood, laws, language? Well, no, we were not. But our differences were not so apparent then. In any case, we took on the job. We would supervise and civilize the lesser breeds. We would make money.

By the end of the Second World War, we were the most powerful and least damaged of the great nations. We also had most of the money. America's hegemony lasted exactly five years. Then the cold and hot wars began.

Our masters would have us believe that all our problems are the fault of the Evil Empire of the East, with its satanic and atheistic religion, ever ready to destroy us in the night. This nonsense began at a time when we had atomic weapons and the Russians did not. They had lost twenty million of their people in the war, and eight million of them before the war, thanks to their neoconservative Mongolian political system. Most important, there was

8

never any chance, then or now, of the money power shifting from New York to Moscow.

What was—and is—the reason for the big scare? Well, the Second War made prosperous the United States, which had been undergoing a depression for a dozen years, and made very rich those magnates and their managers who govern the republic, with many a wink, in the people's name. In order to maintain a general prosperity (and enormous wealth for the few), they decided that we would become the world's policeman, perennial shield against the Mongol hordes.

We shall have an arms race, said one of the high priests, John Foster Dulles, and we shall win it because the Russians will go broke first. We were then put on a permanent wartime economy, which is why close to 90% of the government's revenues are constantly being siphoned off to pay for what is euphemistically called defense.*

As early as 1950, Albert Einstein understood the nature of the rip-off. He said, "The men who possess real power in this country have no intention of ending the cold war." Thirty-five years later, they are still at it, making money while the nation itself declines to eleventh place in world per capita income, to forty-sixth in literacy and so on, until last

---

* [For more details, see pp. 32–33.]

summer [1985] (not suddenly, I fear), we found ourselves close to two trillion dollars in debt. (Now [in 1992] the debt is $4 trillion, with a Bullet, as they say in *Billboard*.)

Then, in the fall, the money power shifted from New York to Tokyo, and that was the end of our empire. Now the long-feared Asiatic colossus takes its turn as world leader, and we—the white race—have become the yellow man's burden. Let us hope that he will treat us more kindly than we treated him.*

In any case, if the foreseeable future is not nuclear, it will be Asiatic, some combination of Japan's advanced technology with China's resourceful landmass. Europe and the United States will then be, simply, irrelevant to the world that matters, and so we come full circle: Europe began as the relatively empty uncivilized Wild West of Asia; then the Western Hemisphere became the Wild West of Europe. Now the sun has set in our West and risen once more in the East.

The British used to say that their empire was obtained in a fit of absentmindedness. They exaggerate, of course. On the other hand, our modern empire was carefully thought out by four men. In 1890, a US Navy captain, Alfred Thayer Mahan, wrote the blue-

---

* Believe it or not, this plain observation was interpreted as a racist invocation of "the Yellow Peril"!

print for the American imperium, *The Influence of Sea Power Upon History, 1660-1783.*

Then Mahan's friend, the historian-geopolitician Brooks Adams, younger brother of Henry, came up with the following formula: "All civilization is centralization. All centralization is economy." He applied the formula in the following syllogism: "Under economical centralization, Asia is cheaper than Europe. The world tends to economic centralization. Therefore, Asia tends to survive and Europe to perish." Ultimately, *that* is why we were in Vietnam.

The amateur historian and professional politician Theodore Roosevelt was much under the influence of Adams and Mahan; he was also their political instrument, most active not so much during his presidency as during the crucial war with Spain, where he can take a good deal of credit for our seizure of the Philippines, which made us a world empire. Finally, Senator Henry Cabot Lodge, Roosevelt's closest friend, kept in line a Congress that had a tendency to forget our holy mission—our manifest destiny—and ask, rather wistfully, for internal improvements.

From the beginning of our republic we have had imperial longings. We took care—as we continue to take care—of the indigenous population. We maintained slavery a bit too long even by a cynical world's tolerant standards. Then, in 1846, we produced our first conquistador, President James K. Polk.

After acquiring Texas, Polk deliberately started a war with Mexico because, as he later told the historian George Bancroft, we had to acquire California. Thanks to Polk, we did. And that is why to this day the Mexicans refer to our southwestern states as "the occupied lands," which Hispanics are now, quite sensibly, filling up.

The case against empire began as early as 1847. Representative Abraham Lincoln did not think much of Polk's war, while Lieutenant Ulysses S. Grant, who fought at Veracruz, said in his memoirs, "The war was an instance of a republic following the bad example of European monarchies, in not considering justice in their desire to acquire additional territory."

He went on to make a causal link, something not usual in our politics then and completely unknown now: "The Southern rebellion was largely the outgrowth of the Mexican War. Nations, like individuals, are punished for their transgressions. We got our punishment in the most sanguinary and expensive war of modern times."

But the empire has always had more supporters than opponents. By 1895 we had filled up our section of North America. We had tried twice—and failed—to conquer Canada.* We had taken everything that we wanted from Mexico. Where next? Well, there was the Caribbean at our front door and the vast Pacific at our back. Enter the Four Horsemen—Mahan, Adams, Roosevelt and Lodge.

The original republic was thought out carefully, and openly, in *The Federalist Papers:* We were not going to have a monarchy, and we were not going to have a democracy. And to this day we have had neither. For two hundred years we have had an oligarchical system in which men of property can do well and the others are on their own.

Or, as Brooks Adams put it, the sole problem of our ruling class is whether to coerce or to bribe the powerless majority. The so-called Great Society bribed; today coercion is very much in the air. Happily, our neoconservatives favor only authoritarian and never totalitarian means of coercion.

Unlike the republic, the empire was worked out largely in secret. Captain Mahan, in a series of lectures delivered at the Naval War College, compared the United States with England. Each was essentially an island

---

* When the British occupied Boston in 1775, Washington struck not at Boston but at Montreal. In 1812, a year before the British burned the White House, we again invaded, unsuccessfully, Canada.

state that could prevail in the world only through sea power.

England had already proved his thesis. Now the United States must do the same. We must build a great navy in order to acquire overseas possessions. Since great navies are expensive, the wealth of new colonies must be used to pay for our fleets. In fact, the more colonies acquired, the more ships; the more ships, the more empire.

Mahan's thesis is agreeably circular. He showed how small England had ended up with most of Africa and all of southern Asia, thanks to sea power. He thought that we should do the same. The Caribbean was our first and easiest target. Then on to the Pacific Ocean, with all its islands. And, finally, to China, which was breaking up as a political entity.

Theodore Roosevelt and Brooks Adams were tremendously excited by this prospect. At the time Roosevelt was a mere police commissioner in New York City, but he had dreams of imperial glory. "He wants to be," snarled Henry Adams, "our Dutch-American Napoleon."

Roosevelt began to maneuver his way toward the heart of power, sea power. With Lodge's help, he got himself appointed assistant secretary of the navy, under a weak secretary and a mild president. Now he was in place to modernize the fleet and to acquire colonies.

Hawaii was annexed. Then a part of Samoa. Finally, colonial Cuba, somehow, had to be liberated from Spain's tyranny. At the Naval War College, Roosevelt declared, "To prepare for war is the most effectual means to promote peace."

How familiar that sounds! But since the United States had no enemies as of June 1897, a contemporary might have remarked that since we were already at peace with everyone, why prepare for war?

Today, of course, we are what he dreamed we would be, a nation armed to the teeth and hostile to everyone. But what with Roosevelt was a design to acquire an empire is for us a means to transfer money from the Treasury to the various defense industries, which in turn pay for the elections of Congress and president.

Our turn-of-the-century imperialists may have been wrong, and I think they were. But they were intelligent men with a plan, and the plan worked. Aided by Lodge in the Senate, Brooks Adams in the press, Admiral Mahan at the Naval War College, the young assistant secretary of the navy began to build up the fleet and look for enemies. After all, as Brooks Adams proclaimed, "war is the solvent." But war with whom? And for what? And where?

At one point England seemed a likely enemy. There was a boundary dispute over

Venezuela, which meant that we could invoke the all-purpose Monroe Doctrine (the invention of John Quincy Adams, Brooks' grandfather). But as we might have lost such a war, nothing happened. Nevertheless, Roosevelt kept on beating his drum: "No triumph of peace," he shouted, "can equal the armed triumph of war." Also: "We must take Hawaii in the interests of the white race."

Even Henry Adams, who found T.R. tiresome and Brooks, his own brother, brilliant but mad, suddenly declared, "In another fifty years...the white race will have to reconquer the tropics by war and nomadic invasion, or be shut up north of the 50th parallel." And so at century's end, our most distinguished ancestral voices were not prophesying but praying for war.

An American warship, the *Maine,* blew up in Havana harbor. We held Spain responsible; thus, we got what John Hay called "a splendid little war." We would liberate Cuba, drive Spain from the Caribbean. As for the Pacific, even before the *Maine* was sunk, Roosevelt had ordered Commodore Dewey and his fleet to the Spanish Philippines—just in case. Spain promptly collapsed, and we inherited its Pacific and Caribbean colonies. Admiral Mahan's plan was working triumphantly.

In time we allowed Cuba the appearance of freedom while holding on to Puerto Rico. Then

President William McKinley, after an in-depth talk with God, decided that we should also keep the Philippines, in order, he said, to Christianize them. When reminded that the Filipinos were Roman Catholics, the president said, Exactly. We must Christianize them.

Although Philippine nationalists had been our allies against Spain, we promptly betrayed them and their leader, Emilio Aguinaldo. As a result it took us several years to conquer the Philippines, and tens of thousands of Filipinos died that our empire might grow.

The war was the making of Theodore Roosevelt. Surrounded by the flower of the American press, he led a group of so-called Rough Riders up a very small hill in Cuba. As a result of this proto-photo opportunity he became a national hero, governor of New York, McKinley's running mate and, when McKinley was killed in 1901, president.

Not everyone liked the new empire. After Manila, Mark Twain thought that the stars and bars of the American flag should be replaced by a skull and crossbones. He also said, "We cannot maintain an empire in the Orient and maintain a republic in America." He was right, of course. But as he was only a writer who said funny things, he was ignored.

The compulsively vigorous Roosevelt defended our war against the Philippine population, and he attacked the likes of Twain.

"Every argument that can be made for the Filipinos could be made for the Apaches," he explained, with his lovely gift for analogy. "And every word that can be said for Aguinaldo could be said for Sitting Bull. As peace, order and prosperity followed our expansion over the land of the Indians, so they'll follow us in the Philippines."

Despite the criticism of the few, the Four Horsemen had pulled it off. The United States was a world empire. And one of the horsemen not only got to be president, but for his pious meddling in the Russo-Japanese conflict, our greatest apostle of war was awarded the Nobel Peace Prize. One must never underestimate Scandinavian wit.

Empires are restless organisms. They must constantly renew themselves; should an empire start leaking energy, it will die. Not for nothing were the Adams brothers fascinated by entropy. By energy. By force.

Brooks Adams, as usual, said the unsayable. "Laws are a necessity, " he declared. "Laws are made by the strongest, and they must and shall be obeyed." Oliver Wendell Holmes, Jr., thought this a wonderful observation, while the philosopher William James came to a similar conclusion, which can also be detected, like an invisible dynamo, at the heart of the novels of his brother Henry.

According to Brooks Adams, "The most difficult problem of modern times is unquestionably how to protect property under popular governments." The Four Horsemen fretted a lot about this. They need not have.

We have never had a popular government in the sense that they feared, nor are we in any danger now. Our only political party has two right wings, one called Republican, the other Democratic. But Henry Adams figured all that out back in the 1890s. "We have a single system," he wrote, and "in that system the only question is the price at which the proletariat is to be bought and sold, the bread and circuses."

But none of this was for public consumption. Publicly, the Four Horsemen and their outriders spoke of the American mission to bring to all the world freedom and peace, through slavery and war if necessary. Privately, their constant fear was that the weak masses might combine one day against the strong few, their natural leaders, and take away their money.

As early as the election of 1876, socialism had been targeted as a vast evil that must never be allowed to corrupt simple American persons. When Christianity was invoked as the natural enemy of those who might limit the rich and their games, the combination of cross and dollar sign proved— and proves—irresistible.

During the first decade of our disagreeable century, the great world fact was the internal collapse of China. Who could pick up the pieces? Britain grabbed Kowloon; Russia was busy in the north; the Kaiser's fleet prowled the China coast; Japan was modernizing itself and biding its time.

Although Theodore Roosevelt lived and died a dedicated racist, the Japanese puzzled him. After they sank the Russian fleet, Roosevelt decided that they were to be respected and feared even though they were our racial inferiors. For those Americans who served in the Second World War, it was an article of faith—as of 1941 anyway—that the Japanese could never win a modern war. Because of their slant eyes, they would not be able to master aircraft. Then they sank our fleet at Pearl Harbor.

Jingoism aside, Brooks Adams was a good analyst. In the 1890s he wrote: "Russia, to survive, must undergo a social revolution internally and/or expand externally. She will try to move into Shansi Province, richest prize in the world. Should Russia and Germany combine..." That was the nightmare of the Four Horsemen.

At a time when simpler folk feared the rise of Germany alone, Brooks Adams saw the world ultimately polarized between Russia and the United States, with China as the common prize. American maritime power versus Russia's landmass. That is why, quite seriously, he wanted to extend the Monroe Doctrine to the Pacific Ocean. For him, "war [was] the ultimate form of economic competition."

We are now at the end of the twentieth century. England, France and Germany have all disappeared from the imperial stage. China is now reassembling itself, and Confucius, greatest of political thinkers, is again at the center of the Middle Kingdom. Japan has the world money power and wants a landmass; China now seems ready to go into business with its ancient enemy.

Wars of the sort that the Four Horsemen enjoyed are, if no longer possible, no longer practical. Today's conquests are shifts of currency by computer and the manufacture of those things that people everywhere are willing to buy.

I have said very little about writers because writers have figured very little in our imperial story. The founders of both republic and empire wrote well: Jefferson and Hamilton, Lincoln and Grant, T.R. and the Adamses. Today public figures can no longer write their own speeches or books, and there is some evidence that they can't read them either.

Yet at the dawn of the empire, for a brief instant, our *professional* writers tried to make a difference. Upton Sinclair and company attacked the excesses of the ruling class. Theodore Roosevelt coined the word "muckraking" to describe what they were doing. He did not mean the word as praise.

Since then a few of our writers have written on public themes, but as they were not taken seriously, they have ended by not taking themselves seriously, at least as citizens of a republic. After all, most writers are paid by universities, and it is not wise to be thought critical of a garrison state which spends so much money on so many campuses.

When Confucius was asked what would be the first thing that he would do if he were to lead the state—his never-to-be-fulfilled dream—he said *rectify the language*. This is wise. This is subtle. As societies grow decadent, the language grows decadent too.

Words are used to disguise, not to illuminate, action: You liberate a city by destroying it. Words are used to confuse, so that at election time people will solemnly vote against their own interests. Finally, words must be so twisted as to justify an empire that has now ceased to exist, much less make sense.

Is rectification of our system possible for us? Henry Adams thought not. In 1910 he wrote: "The whole fabric of society will go to wrack if we really lay hands of reform on our rotten institutions." Then he added, "From top to bottom the whole system is a fraud, all of us know it, laborers and capitalists alike, and all of us are consenting parties to it." Since then, consent has grown frayed; and we have become poor, and our people sullen.

To maintain a thirty-five-year arms race it is necessary to have a fearsome enemy. Not since the invention of the Wizard of Oz have American publicists created anything quite so demented as the idea that the Soviet Union is a monolithic, omnipotent empire with tentacles everywhere on earth, intent on our destruction, which will surely take place unless we constantly imitate it with our war machine and its secret services.*

In actual fact, the Soviet Union is a Second World country with a First World military capacity. Frighten the Russians sufficiently and they might blow us up.

By the same token, as our republic now begins to crack under the vast expense of maintaining a mindless imperial force, we might try to blow them up. Particularly if we had a president who really was a twice-born Christian and believed that the good folks

---

* Now that the Soviet has collapsed, the lies that our secret police and media told us for so many years are coming to light. Remember how, in the 1970s, the CIA was reporting the Soviets' astonishing economic surge.

would all go to heaven (where they were headed anyway), and the bad folks would go where *they* belong. Fortunately, to date, we have had only hypocrites in the White House. But you never can tell.

Even worse than the not-very-likely prospect of nuclear war—deliberate or by accident—is the economic collapse of our society because too many of our resources have been wasted on the military. The Pentagon is like a black hole; what goes in is forever lost to us, and no new wealth is created. Hence, our cities, whose centers are unlivable; our crime rate, the highest in the Western world; a public education system that has given up...you know the litany.

There is now only one way out. The time has come for the United States to make common cause with the Soviet Union. The bringing together of the Soviet landmass (with all its natural resources) and our island empire (with all its technological resources) would be of great benefit to each society, not to mention the world.

Also, to recall the wisdom of the Four Horsemen who gave us our empire, the Soviet Union and our section of North America combined would be a match, industrially and technologically, for the Sino-Japanese axis that will dominate the future just as Japan dominates world trade today. But where the horsemen thought of war as the supreme solvent, we now know that war is worse than useless. Therefore, the alliance of the two great powers of the Northern Hemisphere will double the strength of each and give us, working together, an opportunity to survive, economically, in a highly centralized Asiatic world.*

The Nation
January 11, 1986
(originally a speech given for the benefit of PEN)

---

* The suggestion that the United States and the USSR join forces set alarm bells ringing in Freedom's Land. I was denounced as a Communist. Now, six years later, as I predicted, the Russian states are working out partnerships with us.

The National Security State

Every now and then, usually while shaving, I realize that I have lived through nearly one third of the history of the United States, which proves not how old I am but how young the Republic is. The American empire, which started officially in 1898 with our acquisition of the Philippines, came to a peak in the year 1945, while I was still part of that army which had won us the political and economic mastery of two hemispheres.

If anyone had said to me then that the whole thing would be lost in my lifetime, I would have said it is not possible to lose so much so quickly—without an atomic catastrophe at least. But lose it we have.

Yet, in hindsight, I can see that our ending was implicit in our beginning. When Japan surrendered, the United States was faced with a choice: Either disarm, as we had done in the past, and enjoy the prosperity that comes from releasing so much wealth and energy to the private sector, or maintain our-selves on a full military basis, which would mean a tight control not only over our allies and such conquered provinces as West Ger-many, Italy and Japan but over the economic—which is to say the political—lives of the American people.

As Charles E. Wilson, a businessman and politician of the day, said as early as 1944, "Instead of looking to disarmament and unpreparedness as a safeguard against war, a thoroughly discredited doctrine, let us try the opposite: full preparedness according to a continuing plan."

The accidental president, Harry Truman, bought this notion. Although Truman campaigned in 1948 as an heir to Roosevelt's New Deal, he had a "continuing plan." Henry Wallace* was onto it, as early as: "Yesterday, March 12, 1947, marked a turning point in American history, [for] it is not a Greek crisis that we face, it is an American crisis. Yesterday, President Truman...proposed, in effect, America police Russia's every border. There is no regime too reactionary for us provided it stands in Russia's expansionist path. There is no country too remote to serve as the scene of a contest which may widen until it becomes a world war."

But how to impose this? The Republican leadership did not like the state to be the master of the country's economic life while, of

---

* [Henry Wallace (1888–1965), a vice-president under FDR (1941–45), was the Progressive Party candidate for president in 1948.]

the Democrats, only a few geopoliticians, like Dean Acheson* found thrilling the prospect of a military state, to be justified in the name of a holy war against something called communism in general and Russia in particular. The fact that the Soviet Union was no military or economic threat to us was immaterial. It must be made to appear threatening so that the continuing plan could be set in motion in order to create that national security state in which we have been living for the past forty years.

What is the national security state? Well, it began, officially, with the National Security Act of 1947; it was then implemented in January 1950 when the National Security Council produced a blueprint for a new kind of country, unlike anything that the United States had ever known before.

This document, known as NSC–68 for short, and declassified only in 1975, committed—and still, fitfully, commits—us to the following program:

First, never negotiate, ever, with Russia. This could not last forever; but the obligatory bad faith of US-USSR meetings still serves the continuing plan.

Second, develop the hydrogen bomb, so that when the Russians finally develop an

---

* [Dean Acheson (1893–1971) was secretary of state under Truman and one of the prime authors of the Marshall Plan, the Truman Doctrine and NATO.]

atomic bomb we will still not have to deal with that enemy without which the national security state cannot exist.

Third, rapidly build up conventional forces.

Fourth, put through a large increase in taxes to pay for all of this.

Fifth, mobilize the entire American society to fight this terrible specter of communism.

Sixth, set up a strong alliance system, directed by the United States (this became NATO).

Seventh, make the people of Russia our allies, through propaganda and CIA derring-do, in this holy adventure—hence the justification for all sorts of secret services that are in no way responsible to the Congress that funds them, and so in violation of the old Constitution.

Needless to say, the blueprint, the continuing plan, was not openly discussed at the time. But, one by one, the major political players of the two parties came around. Senator Arthur Vandenburg, Republican, told Truman that if he really wanted all those weapons and all those high taxes to pay for them, he had better "scare hell out of the American people."

Truman obliged, with a series of speeches beginning October 23, 1947, about the Red Menace endangering France and Italy; he also instituted loyalty oaths for federal employees;

and his attorney general published a list of dissident organizations (on December 4, 1947).

The climate of fear has been maintained, more or less zealously, by Truman's successors, with the brief exception of Dwight Eisenhower, who in a belated fit of conscience at the end of his presidency warned us against the military-industrial complex that had, by then, established permanent control over the state.

The cynicism of this coup d'état was breathtaking. Officially we were doing nothing but trying to preserve freedom for ourselves and our allies from a ruthless enemy that was everywhere monolithic and all-powerful. Actually, the real enemy were those national security statesmen who had so dexterously hijacked the country, establishing military conscription in peacetime, overthrowing governments that did not please them, and finally keeping all but the very rich docile and jittery by imposing income taxes that theoretically went as high as 90 percent. That is quite an achievement in a country at peace.

We can date from January 1950 the strict governmental control of our economy and the gradual erosion of our liberties, all in order to benefit the economic interest of what is never, to put it tactfully, a very large group—defense spending is money- but not labor-intensive. Fortunately, all bad things must come to an end. Our huge indebtedness has made the maintenance of the empire a nightmare; and the day Japan stops buying our Treasury bonds, the troops and the missiles will all come home to a highly restless population.

Now that I have defined the gloomy prospect, what solutions do I have? I shall make five proposals. First, limit presidential election campaigns to eight weeks. That is what most civilized countries do, and all democratic ones are obliged to do. Allow no paid political ads. We might then entice that half of the electorate which never votes to vote.

Second, the budget: The press and the politicians constantly falsify the revenues and disbursements of the federal government. How? By wrongly counting Social Security contributions and expenditures as a part of the federal budget.

Social Security is an independent, slightly profitable income-transferring trust fund, which should be factored out of federal revenue and federal spending. Why do the press and the politicians conspire to give us this distorted view of the budget? Because neither they nor their owners want the public to know how much of its tax money goes for a war that does not exist.

As a result, Federal Reserve chairman Alan Greenspan could say in the spring of 1988, and with a straight face, that there are only two options for a serious attack on the deficit.

One is to raise taxes. The other is to reduce the entitlement programs like Social Security and Medicare. He did not mention the defense budget. He did not acknowledge that the so-called entitlements come from a special fund. But then, he is a disciple of Ayn Rand.

In actual fact, close to 90 percent of the disbursements of the federal government go for what is laughingly known as "defense." This is how: In 1986, the gross revenue of the government was $794 billion. Of that amount, $294 billion were Social Security contributions, which should be subtracted from the money available to the national security state. That leaves $500 billion. Subsequent budgets show different figures but similar proportions.

Of the $500 billion, $286 billion went to defense; $12 billion for foreign arms to our client states; $8 billion to $9 billion to energy, which means, largely, nuclear weapons; $27 billion for veterans' benefits, the sad and constant reminder of the ongoing empire's recklessness; and, finally, $142 billion for interest on loans that were spent, over the past forty years, to keep the national security state at war, hot or cold.

So, of 1986's $500 billion in revenue, $475 billion was spent on National Security business. Of that amount, we will never know how much was "kicked back" through political action committees and so-called soft money to subsidize candidates and elections. Other federal spending, incidentally, came to $177 billion in 1986 (guarding presidential candidates, cleaning the White House), which was about the size of the deficit, since only $358 billion was collected in taxes.

It is obvious that if we are to avoid an economic collapse, defense spending must be drastically reduced. But it is hard to reduce a budget that the people are never told about. The first politician who realizes why those politicians who appear to run against the government always win, could not only win himself but be in a position to rid us of the national security state—which is what people truly hate.

"Internal improvements" was the slogan of Henry Clay's popular movement.* A neo-Clayite could sweep the country if he wanted seriously to restore the internal plant of the country rather than invade Honduras or bob expensively about the Persian Gulf or overthrow a duly elected government in Nicaragua while running drugs (admittedly, the CIA's only margin of profit).

Third, as part of our general retrenchment, we should withdraw from NATO. Western Europe is richer and more populous than America.

---

* [Famed for his oratory and his ability to forge compromises, Henry Clay (1777–1852) was a senator, secretary of state, speaker of the House of Representatives and presidential candidate.]

If it cannot defend itself from an enemy who seems to be falling apart even faster than we are, then there is nothing that we, proud invaders of Grenada, can effectively do.

I would stop all military aid to the Middle East. This would oblige the hardliners in Israel to make peace with the Palestinians. We have supported Israel for forty years. No other minority in the history of the United States has ever extorted so much Treasury money for its Holy Land as the Israeli lobby, and it has done this by making a common cause with the national security state. Each supports the other. I would have us cease to pay for either.

Fourth, we read each day about the horrors of drug abuse, the murder of policemen, the involvement of our own government in drug running, and so on. We are all aware that organized crime has never been richer nor the society more demoralized. What is the solution? I would repeal every prohibition against the sale and use of drugs, because it is these prohibitions that have caused the national corruption, not to mention most of the addiction.

Since the American memory has a span of about three days, I will remind you that in 1919 alcohol was prohibited in the United States. In 1933 Prohibition was repealed because not only had organized crime expanded enormously but so had alcoholism. What did not work then does not work now. But we never learn, which is part of our national charm.

Repeal would mean that there is no money for anyone in selling drugs. That's the end of the playground pusher. That's the end of organized crime, which has already diversified and is doing very nicely in banking, films, and dry cleaning. Eventually, repeal will mean the end of mass drug addiction. As there will always be alcoholics, there will always be drug addicts, but not to today's extent. It will be safe to walk the streets because the poor will not rob you to pay for their habit.*

Fifth, as I have noted above, the American empire ended the day the money power shifted from New York to Tokyo and we became, for the first time since 1914, a debtor nation. Since then, we have become the largest debtor country in history. I suggested a number of things that might be done, some of which I've again mentioned.

But, above all, I see our economic survival inextricably bound up with that of our neighbor in the Northern Hemisphere, the Soviet Union. As the two klutzes of the north, each unable to build a car anyone wants to drive, we deserve each other.

---

* I called for the legalization of drugs pretty much in these same words on the op-ed page of *The New York Times*, September 26, 1970. Since then, many voices have joined mine.

In a speech at Gorbachev's anti-nuclear forum in Moscow, I quoted a Japanese minister of trade who said that Japan would still be number one in the next century. Then, tactlessly he said that the United States will be Japan's farm and Western Europe its boutique. A Russian got up and asked, "What did he say about us?" I said that they were not mentioned but, if they did not get their act together, they would end up as ski instructors.

It is my impression that the Russians are eager to be Americans, but, thanks to the brainwashing of the national security state's continuing plan, Americans have a built-in horror of the Evil Empire, which the press and the politicians have kept going for forty years.* Happily, our national security state is in the red, in more ways than one. Time for a change?

> *The Nation*
> June 4, 1988
> *(originally given as a speech at the*
> *National Press Club)*

---

* The press, which should know better, is of no help. The Iran-Contra hearings were a sudden dramatic confrontation between the real government of the United States, as represented by Ollie North et al., and the cosmetic government. Ollie told us as much. But no one got the point.

Cue The Green God, Ted

There has not been a political debate in the United States since the one that ended with the Japanese attack on Pearl Harbor. From September 1939 to December 7, 1941, the ruling class of the United States was split between those who would join the Allies in their war against Hitler and those who would stay out. For over two years there was fierce argument in Congress, the press, the schools.

At my school, Exeter, there was a sharp division between the isolationists, known as America Firsters, and the interventionists. True to the populist tradition in which I was brought up, I was isolationist. Then, or as Lincoln once so bleakly put it, *and the war came;* and I enlisted in the Army, age 17.

Since the victory of 1945, the United States, as befits the leader of something called "the free world," has fought open and unsuccessful wars in Korea and Vietnam; and relatively covert wars in Cambodia, Laos, the Caribbean, Central America, Africa, Chile, the Middle East, etc. In almost every case, our overwhelming commitment to freedom, democracy and human rights has required us to support those regimes that would deny freedom, democracy and human rights to their own people.

We justify our affection for fascist (or, to be cozy, authoritarian) regimes because each and every one of them is a misty-eyed convert to our national religion, which is anticommunism. Then, once our dictator is in place, we echo Andy Hardy: Hey, kids, let's put on an election! And so, in the presence of cold-eyed avatars of Tammany and Daley, our general on the spot does.

To their credit, our rulers don't often bore us with tortured rationalizations or theological nit-picking. They don't have to. Since we have no political parties and no opposition media, there is always a semblance of "consensus" for these wars. Congress funds the Pentagon, which then responds to the national security state's directives to overthrow an Arbenz here or a Sihanouk there or—why not?—devastate a neutral country like Cambodia to show how tall we can stand in all our marvelously incredible credibility.

Voices of dissent are either silenced or marginalized, while known apostates of the national religion are either demonized or trivialized. Meanwhile, no one has noticed that the national security state, in its zeal to bring the national religion to all nations, has now deprived us of our original holy text—our Old Testament—the Constitution.

Every war that we have fought since 1945 has been by executive (or National Security

Council) order. Since only Congress may declare war, these wars have all been in violation of the Constitution. To the House of Representatives was assigned, uniquely, the power of the purse. But, in thrall to those religious wars that we forever fight, our debts are now so great that Congress dares not prepare a proper budget.

So the power of the purse has been replaced by a ridiculous formula, involving a blind arbitrary cutting of the budget should Federal waste exceed a certain arbitrary figure. Although the most militant of our national religionists enjoy calling themselves conservatives, they have not managed to conserve either the letter or the spirit of the Old Testament.

For some time knowledgeable foreigners have found it difficult to talk about much of anything to Americans because we appear to know so little about much of anything. History of any kind is a closed book to us. Geography is no longer taught in most public schools. Foreign languages make everyone's head ache—anyway, *they* all know English.

As for politics, that's simple: It's either *us* (what the silver-tongued felon Spiro Agnew, or his wordsmith William Safire, so memorably dubbed "the greatest nation in the country") or *them*—foreigners who envy us our vast choice of detergents, our freedom to repeat as loudly as we want the national prayers, our alabaster cities to which, we tell ourselves, they can't wait to emigrate.

On the other hand, the average American, when it comes to his own welfare, is very shrewd indeed. He knows that we are in an economic decline and that our quality of life, though better than that of Russia (all that really matters, our priests hum softly) is noticeably lousy. But the reasons for our decline are never made clear because the corporate ownership of the country has absolute control of the populist pulpit—"the media"—as well as of the schoolroom.

David Hume's celebrated 1758 *Of the First Principles of Government* has never been more to the point than now:

> Nothing appears more surprising to those who consider human affairs with a philosophical eye than the easiness with which the many are governed by the few, and the implicit submission with which men resign their own sentiments and passions to those of their rulers. When we inquire by what means this wonder is effected, we shall find that, as force is always on the side of the governed, the governors have nothing to support them but opinion. It is, therefore, on opinion only that government is founded, and this maxim extends to the most despotic and most military governments as well as to the most free and most popular.

The corporate grip on opinion in the United States is one of the wonders of the Western world. No First World country has ever managed to eliminate so entirely from its media all objectivity—much less dissent. Of course, it is possible for any citizen with time to spare, and a canny eye, to work out what is actually going on, but for the many there is no time, and the network news is the only news even though it may not be news at all but only a series of flashing fictions intended, like the avowed commercials, to keep docile huddled masses, keep avid for products addled consumers.

I seldom watch television. But when I do set out to twirl the dial, it is usually on Sunday, when our corporate rulers address us from their cathode pulpit. Seedy Washington journalists, sharp-eyed government officials who could not dispose of a brand-new car in Spokane, think-tank employees, etiolated from too long residence 'neath flat rocks, and always, always, Henry Kissinger, whose destruction of so many Asians and their once-charming real estate won him a prize for peace from the ironists of outer Europe.

The level of the chat on those programs is about as low as it is possible to get without actually serving the viewers gin. The opinion expressed ranges from conservative to reactionary to joyous neofascist. There is even, in William Safire, an uncloseted anti-Gentile.

I was once placed between two waxworks on a program where one of the pair was solemnly identified as a "liberal"; appropriately, he seemed to have been dead for some time, while the conservative had all the vivacity of someone on speed. For half an hour it is the custom of this duo to "crossfire" clichés of the sort that would have got them laughed out of the Golden Branch Debating Society at Exeter.

On air, I identified the conservative as a liberal and vice versa. The conservative fell into the trap. "No, no!" he hyperventilated. "I'm the conservative!" (What on earth they think these two words mean no one will ever know.) It was the liberal who got the point; from beyond, as it were, the tomb he moaned, "He's putting us on."

I have been involved in television since the early 1950s, when it ceased to be a novelty and became the principal agent for the simultaneous marketing of consumer goods and of national security state opinion. Although I thought I knew quite a bit about the ins and outs of the medium, I now know a lot more, thanks to Ben H. Bagdikian's *The Media Monopoly* and *Manufacturing Consent*, a study of "the political economy of the mass media," by Edward S. Herman and Noam Chomsky.

These two studies demonstrate exactly how the few manipulate opinion. To begin with: The average American household keeps the set throbbing seven hours a day. This means the average American has watched 350,000 commercials by age 17.

Since most opinion is now controlled by twenty-nine corporations—due to be at least one fewer if Time-Warner or Paramount-Time or, most chilling of all, Nation-Time comes to pass, one can then identify those twenty-nine CEOs as a sort of politburo or college of cardinals, in strict charge of what the people should and should not know.

They also select the Presidents and the Congresses or, to be precise, they determine what the politicians may talk about at election time—that famed agenda that never includes the interesting detail that, in peacetime, close to 90% of the Federal revenue goes to war [see pp. 32–33 for details].

Although AIDS *can* be discussed as a means of hitting out at unpopular minorities, the true epidemic can never be discussed: the fact that every fourth American now alive will die of cancer. This catastrophe is well kept from the public by the tobacco companies, the nuclear power companies (with their bungled waste disposal) and other industries that poison the earth, so that corporate America may enjoy the freedom to make money without the slightest accountability to those they are killing.

The invention of the talk show on television was, at first, a most promising development. Admittedly, no one very radical would ever be allowed on, but a fair range of opinion could be heard, particularly as the Vietnam War began to go bad. On the original *Today* show, Hugh Downs and I would talk off and on for an hour as news, weather, commercials floated lazily by.

But Hazel Bishop, an obscure lipstick company, changed all that. The firm began running commercials not linked to specific programs and it was soon determined that the thirty-second commercial duplicates exactly the attention span of the average viewer. Therefore, no in-depth interview can last for more than seven minutes; three minutes is considered optimum.

Recently, I found myself confronting the amiable Pat Sajak. I was all set to do what I think of as my inventing-the-wheel-in-seven-minutes (why what's wrong is wrong and what to do) when my energy level crashed. I did say that if you wanted to know what the ownership of the country wants you to know, tune in to *Nightline* and listen to Ted Koppel and his guests. The effect of this bit of information must have been surreal. Since no voices other than those of the national consensus are heard, how could a viewer know that there are any other viewpoints?

I was made aware of the iron rules in 1968, when William F. Buckley Jr. and I had our first live chat on ABC at the Republican Convention in Miami Beach. I was billed as the conservative; he as the pro-crypto—or was it the other way around? Anyway, we were hired to play the opinion game in order to divert the audience from the issues.

Buckley Junior's idea of a truly deep in-depth political discussion is precisely that of corporate America's. First, the Democrat must say that the election of a Republican will lead to a depression. Then the Republican will joyously say, Ahhahhhhh, but the Democrats always lead us into war!

After a few minutes of this, *my* attention span snapped. I said that there was no difference at all between the two parties because the same corporations paid for both, usually with taxpayers' money, tithed, as it were, from the faithful and then given to "defense," which in turn passes it on to those candidates who will defend the faith.

With that bit of news for the national audience, I revealed myself not only as an apostate to the national religion; I came close to revealing what I really am: a dedicated anti-anti-communist, a category far more vile to the true believer than a mere Communist. Although my encounters with Buckley Junior got ABC its highest ratings, I was seen no more at election times.

Last year, Peter Jennings proposed to ABC that, for old times' sake, it might be a good idea to have me on. "No," he was told, "He'll just be outrageous."

In 1972 the future Supreme court Justice Lewis Powell wrote the US Chamber of Commerce proposing that they "buy the top academic reputations in the country to add credibility to corporate studies and give business a stronger voice on the campuses." One wonders, stronger than what? But the advice was taken. Also, as corollary, keep off prime-time television those who do not support corporate America.

During the 1960s and the early 1970s I used, once a year, to do a "state of the union" analysis on David Susskind's non-network, non-prime-time television program. Many people watched. In the summer before the 1976 presidential election, Susskind wanted to produce a series of one-hour interviews with the twenty or so leading candidates of the two parties. For one hour I would question each candidate about politics, history, economics—whatever came up. Since I favored no candidate and neither party, I could not be said to be partisan.

PBS agreed that this sort of program was precisely why PBS had been founded and funded. All the candidates, save President Ford, affected delight. As we prepared for the first program, the head of PBS affiliate WNET, Jay Iselin, canceled the series without explanation.

Then the intrepid producer, Hillard Elkins, took over. He had "a good relationship" with Home Box Office, which was "hungry for product." HBO manifested delight in having its hunger so cheaply sated. Then, just before the first taping, Andrew Heiskell, the overall capo of Time-Life-HBO, canceled us.

In due course, I was advised that it was not in the national (that is, corporate) interest for so many *expensive* presidential candidates to be questioned by me in a—what was the phrase?—"nonstructured format." Now, of course, with the megacorporate ownership of the media becoming more and more concentrated in fewer and fewer hands, structure is total, indeed totalitarian, and the candidates can no longer be discerned through the heavy blizzard of thirty-second spots.

Currently, the principal dispenser of the national religion is Ted Koppel, a very smooth bishop indeed. Fairness & Accuracy in Reporting—noble, doomed enterprise—had a study made of just who appeared as Koppel's guests during a forty-month period from 1985 to 1988. White male establishment types predominated.

Henry Kissinger (Koppel's guru and a long-time cardinal in the national security state's curia) and Alexander Haig (by his own admission, in one of many moments of confusion at the White House, "a vicar") each appeared fourteen times, the maximum for any guest. Yet the cardinal's views on almost any subject are already known to anyone who might be interested in looking at *Nightline,* while Haig's opinions have never interested anybody in the course of a long busy career climbing ladders so that he could be close to those with power in order...to be close to them.

The next two champ guests, weighing in at twelve appearances each, were the mendacious Elliott Abrams (Koppel assumes that although Abrams will lie to Congress, he won't lie to Koppel) and Jerry Falwell, a certified voice of God whose dolorous appearance suggests a deep, almost personal grief that the Thirteenth and Fourteenth Amendments to the Constitution are not yet repealed. Most of the other guests are hired guns for the national security state.

The Koppel explanation for this bizarre repertory company is that, well, they are the folks who are running the country and so that's why they're on. Well, yes, Ted, that *is* why they're on, but there are other more interesting and more learned—even disinterested—

voices in the land and, in theory, they should be heard, too.

But theory is not practice in bravery's home. Of semidissenters, only Jesse Jackson and Studs Terkel have been honored with solo interviews with the bishop, who insists, by the way, that the guest face not him but a camera in another room, preferably in another city, with an earphone but no monitor. Good television one-upmanship.

To my amazement, just before Mikhail Gorbachev spoke at the United Nations, on December 7, 1988, I was asked to contribute a tiny prerecorded (and thus easily edited) cameo. I suppose that I was asked because I had attended Gorbachev's famous antinuclear forum in Moscow two years earlier. I spoke to a camera. I predicted, accurately, that Gorbachev would say that Russia was unilaterally disarming, and that we were now dangerously close to peace.

To the question, What will the United States do without The Enemy?—a pretty daring question from those whose livelihood depends on the demonizing of Russia and Communism—I said that, thanks to television, a new demon can be quickly installed. Currently, the Arabs are being thoroughly demonized by the Israel lobby while the Japanese are being, somewhat more nervously, demonized by elements of the corporate state. But neither will do as a long-term devil because the Arabs are too numerous (and have too much oil) while the Japanese will simply order us to stop it; should we disobey them, they will buy the networks and show us many hours of the soothing tea ceremony.

I suggested that the new devil will be the threat to our ecosphere, and the new world god, Green. None of this was used, of course, but a man who writes Russians-Are-Coming thrillers was shown, frowning with intense anguish at, What, *what!* does it all mean? Because you godda be real careful with these guys. Fine show, Ted.

The unloved American empire is now drifting into history on a sea of red ink, as I predicted (on pp. 7–25), to the fury of the few and the bewilderment of the many. Thanks to money wasted in support of the national religion, our quality of life is dire, and although our political institutions work smoothly for the few, the many hate them; hence the necessity of every corporate candidate for President to run against the government, which is, of course, the corporate state—good fun.

In due course, something on the order of the ethnic rebellions in the Soviet Union or even of the people's uprising in China will take place here. Too few have ripped off too many for too long. Opinion can no longer disguise the contradiction at the heart of conservative-corporate opinion. The corporate few are free to do what they will to customers and environment, while the many are losing their freedoms at a rapid rate.

The Supreme Court, the holy office of the national religion, in upholding the principle of preventive detention, got rid of due process not long ago, and now the Court is busily working its way through the Bill of Rights, producing, as it goes, a series of bright, crackling autos-da-fé.

Significantly, our prison population is now among the world's largest. Certainly it is right up there, per capita, with the Soviet Union and the Republic of South Africa.* Now the few are proposing that if the war budget is to be, tragically, reduced, the army camps—perfect symbolism—can be used to house our criminal population, particularly weak-fibered drug users.

Thus do the few now declare open war on the many, as millions of citizens are now liable to mandatory blood, urine and lie-detector tests, while an electronic bracelet has been invented that will make it possible to track its wearer wherever he goes. Theoretically, half a nation can now monitor the movements of the

---

* [By now we've passed them both, as noted on p. 64.]

other half. Better we enslave ourselves, the priests chant, than *they* do.

Lately, the language of government, always revealing, grows more and more fierce and commanding (due to so many wars lost? so much money wasted?), and military metaphors abound as czars lead all-out wars on drugs. Yet, at the risk of causing both offense and embarrassment among even the not-so-faithful, I feel obliged to say that I do not accept the authority of any state—much less one founded as was ours upon the free fulfillment of each citizen—to forbid me, or anyone, the use of drugs, cigarettes, alcohol, sex with a consenting partner or, if one is a woman, the right to an abortion. I take these rights to be absolute and should the few persist in their efforts to dominate the private lives of the many, I recommend force as a means of changing their minds.

Meanwhile, let us hope that opinion will respond to recent events. For instance, despite millions of dollars spent in the 1988 presidential election on trying—successfully—to obscure every political issue while demonstrating—unsuccessfully—that there was a dramatic difference between Dukakis and Bush, 50 percent of the American electorate refused to vote. When a majority boycotts a political system, its days are numbered. The many are now ready for a change. The few are demoralized.

Fortunately, the Messiah is at hand: the Green God. Everyone on earth now worships him. Soon there will be a worldwide Green movement, and the establishment of a world-wide state, which the few will take over, thus enslaving us all while forgetting to save the planet. That is the worst-case scenario. The best? Let the many create a *new* few.

The Nation
August 7/14, 1989

Time for a People's Convention

November 18, 1991. Despite jet lag, I find myself, half-asleep, making a speech in a nineteenth-century auditorium in Pittsburgh. I stand behind a lectern at stage left, blinded by film and television lights. At stage right stands the youthful "Bob Roberts," played by Tim Robbins, who is also the director, writer, producer of this film.

We are fictional characters. I am the incumbent liberal Senator from Pennsylvania; he is the challenger. "Bob" is a self-made millionaire turned pop singer, now turned politician. He is a sort of David Duke but without the luggage of a lurid past. He will win the election in the film, *Bob Roberts,* opening September 1, 1992.

I have a weird sense that I have done all this before. Certainly, the hall is familiar, even to the entire text of the Gettysburg Address in giant gold letters above the stage. Then I realize that "I" have been through all this some weeks earlier. Only I was Harris Wofford and "Bob Roberts" was Dick Thornburgh and they, too, spoke in the same hall. That time Wofford won; this time he—"I"—loses. Then as my peroration resounds, I realize that I have never actually been in Pittsburgh before and that my familiarity with the hall is because of CNN—or was it C-Span?

Once I had finished my work as co-star, I moved on to Dartmouth where I spent a week in Hanover, New Hampshire, chatting with faculty and students. But, again, unreality kept breaking in. My first morning in Hanover I looked out the bedroom window and for a moment I thought I was back at my old school, Exeter, from which I had graduated a half-century earlier, unless a recurrent nightmare runs true to course, in which case I did *not* graduate but have spent fifty dusty years trying, unsuccessfully, to make up a failed math test.

Once awake, I found that my old friend déjà vu was back in town as a half-dozen hopeless presidential candidates were going through their quadrennial paces. In 1982 I had run against one of them, Jerry Brown, in California and lost a Senate primary election. Now he was making my old speeches. Should I warn him not to? No. Meanwhile, New Hampshire is in deep depression—shops out of business, banks failed, real estate belly-up, and everywhere the newly unemployed, looking for work where there is none.

From Dartmouth to Miami, and a firsthand look at the collapse of Pan American in its capital city. Local television devoted a great deal of time to the 7,500 workers suddenly let go, while stunned passengers crowded the ticket counters in order to read the scribbled message: "All Pan Am flights canceled"—forever. I thought of the arrogant Juan Trippe, who had founded the airline at about the same time that my father was founding what was to become TWA, now near bankruptcy.

I am definitely dreaming, I decided, and drove on to Key West, which I had not seen since my last visit to Tennessee Williams, thirty years earlier. German and French families crowded Duval Street, taking advantage of the cheap (ever cheaper as I write) dollar. I felt like a ghost who has been granted a day's visit to the future. I split for limbo, my home city of Washington, D.C., where I was due to address the National Press Club.

The usual efforts (led this time by the ever-winsome Marianne Means) had been made to block my appearance but, as usual, they had failed. Apparently I am "outrageous," a word never exactly defined, though—from what I can tell—it appears to mean that as I say what I think about our political system and as I think a lot more about it than any of those journalists who are paid to present an irreal picture of these bad times, I cause a degree of outrage if not, as I would hope, rage.

This is the third time in thirty years that I have talked to the press club. Before me, my father addressed the club; before him, my grandfather. In a way, this is a family affair, but lately the family's hometown seems to have fallen apart.

That morning I strolled from the Willard Hotel toward the Capitol. Burnt-out buildings just off Pennsylvania Avenue; burnt-out people on the avenue—and elsewhere, too. It was like the spring of 1932, when jobless veterans of World War I marched by the thousands on the capital and set up a camp on the Anacostia Flats. They wanted a bonus. On June 17, I drove with my grandfather to the Senate. They stoned his car.

Ever since, I have always known that the famous "it" which can't happen here will happen here, and last month as I walked through my home city, "it" seemed ever closer to hand, and we are now in a prerevolutionary time. Hence, the emphasis in the media on the breakup of the Soviet Union and Yugoslavia, or of anything other than the breakdown, if not breakup, of the United States and its economy.

Just now, a month later, I watched on television as angry workers stormed through the streets of what I took to be Moscow, until CNN identified the city as New York and the workers as members of one of our few labor unions—construction workers, I think, protesting lack of work, hope.

Like a ghost—but this time from the future—I tried to explain to the press club what it is they do that they don't know they do. I quote David Hume: The Few are able to control the Many only through Opinion.* In the eighteenth century, Opinion was dispensed from pulpit and schoolroom. Now the media are in place to give us Opinion that has been manufactured in the boardrooms of those corporations—once national, now international—that control our lives.

Naturally, this sounded to my audience like the old conspiracy theory. Later, I was asked if I actually thought that Kay Graham and Larry Tisch really told the news departments of *The Washington Post* and CBS what to tell us. I said, Yes, of course, they do on occasion, but in everyday practice they don't need to give instructions because everyone who works for them thinks exactly alike on those economic issues that truly matter.

I even mentioned the unmentionable, the ruling class. I noted that those members who were not going to inherit money are sent like Bush to Andover and me to Exeter—two schools for the relatively brainy. Those who will inherit money (e.g. the late Nelson Rockefeller) go to Groton or St. Paul's, where, in order not to grow up to become dissolute

---

* [See the quote on p. 40.]

wastrels, they will be taught useful hobbies, like stamp or people collecting.

This sort of education insures that everyone so educated will tend to think alike. The few who break ranks are—what else?—outrageous. In any case, the indoctrination of the prep schools alone is usually quite enough to create a uniformity of ruling-class opinion when it comes to the rights of property. Since our corporate state is deeply democratic, there are always jobs available to middle-class careerists willing to play the game.

Almost forty years ago, I heard Secretary of State John Foster Dulles say that of course our foreign policy (as outlined in the then-secret National Security Council Memorandum 68) would lead to an arms race with the Soviet Union but that, as we were richer, they would cave in first. Dulles was right. They did. But he had not taken into account the economic cost to us or, worse, that in the process we would lose the old Republic and its Constitution, so revered by its current destroyers.

Political decadence occurs when the forms that a state pretends to observe are known to be empty of all meaning. Who does not publicly worship the Constitution? Who, in practice, observes it at all? Congress has only two great powers under the Constitution: the power to declare war and the power of the purse. The first has been relinquished to the Executive; the second has drowned in a red sea.

The Supreme Court is no longer the Executive's equal. Rather, it is the Executive's tool. The White House's open coaching of the unqualified Clarence Thomas for a place on the Court made it dramatically clear that the Court now acts as a nine-member legal council to the Executive, its principal function the validation of Executive decrees. The current Court has also displayed a startling dislike of the American people, and the joy with which the nine nullities chop away at our Bill of Rights is a marvel to behold.

But then the hatred of those *inside* the fabled Beltway for those *outside* has now—what else?—created a true hatred on the part of the Many for the Few who govern them, or appear to govern, since the actual decision makers—and paymasters—are beyond anyone's reach, out there in the boardrooms of the world.

In the absence of true political debate, we have what I think of as the Sunday zoo on television. Here journalists and politicians gaze at one another thorough the bars of received Opinion and chatter about "process," a near-meaningless word in these parts. Recently I watched Richard Darman, Bush's budget director, gabble to Messrs. Evans and Novak about the deficit. To my amazement, the defense budget was actually mentioned by Evans. Apparently the Brookings Institution had daringly suggested that if a few hundred dollars were cut, we would still be able to support with our swift nuclear sword the "democracy" of Tonga.

But although the defense budget continues to be the cancer that is killing our body politic, it may not be dealt with at any length by the media, and Darman was swift to create the necessary diversion: "Entitlements!" he moaned right on cue. "If only we could get *them* on the table." He shook his head in despair at the trillions of dollars that we waste on free dentures and on the financing in luxury of profligate unwed mothers.

Now it is wonderfully ironic for anyone to complain about what the zoo calls "people programs" because, wasteful or not, there aren't many. But no one can point this out on television because both journalists and politicians are hired by the same people and behind those people is the corporate wealth of the country, which requires that the budget be faked.

The famous entitlements consist largely of disbursements for Social Security, and although Social Security contributions are always counted as part of the federal revenue, they are not. Social Security is a separate trust fund whose income and outgo have *nothing* to do with the actual budget [see p. 31].

If Social Security payments are not counted as revenue, the government is currently spending $1.1 trillion a year, while taking in only $726 billion from taxes. The real national debt is about $4 trillion; in 1980 it was a "mere" $1 trillion.

It is true that the Pentagon itself gets less money these days than it used to, but "defense" or war-related matters—debt service (mostly on money borrowed for war), foreign aid, nuclear energy and payments to the true victims of our wars, the veterans—still accounts for most federal expenditures and deficits.* Recent bulletin from Governor Bill Clinton: In 1990, for the first time, the cost of servicing the debt was equal to the amount of money appropriated for the Pentagon proper.

From time to time it is shyly suggested that taxes be raised—for individuals but never for corporations. To those who maintain that our political life is not controlled by corporations, let me offer a statistical proof of ownership— the smoking gun, in fact. In 1950, 44 percent of federal revenues came from individual taxpayers and 28 percent from a tax on corporate profits. In 1991, 37 percent came from individuals and only 8 percent from the corporations. The rest, of course, is borrowed.

---

* [For details, see pp. 32–33.]

Once Bush's only fiscal notion becomes law and the capital gains tax is eliminated, the work of corporate America will be complete, and the ownership will have ceased to support the United States. Naturally, should a badly run company like Chrysler go bust, the American people will be expected to pay for managerial mistakes.

In any case, let it be solemnly noted that during the forty years of the national security state, corporate America not only collected most of the federal revenue for "defense" but, in the process, reduced its share of federal taxes by twenty percentage points. Was this a conspiracy? No. They all think alike. Yes. They all think alike.

Since it is unlikely that Japan and Germany will continue to buy our Treasury bonds, how will the ownership pay for itself? Well, we could always renege on servicing the debt, but as Richard Nixon would say, *that would be the easy way* (and will, alas, be taken). The sublime way, which will be taken by the next administration, will be to sell off that 31 percent of the United States that is held by the federal government in our name. This fire sale will be highly popular with the buyers, but it will be odd for Americans to have so little real estate to call their own.

When I was last at the National Press Club, Opinion makers were mildly interested in overruns at the Defense Department. There was to be an investigation, and John Tower would be in place to make sure that nothing untoward was discovered. But Dick Cheney got the job instead, and there have been no meaningful investigations on his watch.

Meanwhile, the much discussed savings and loan "bailout" is not possible. In current dollars and including service-connected veteran benefits, the cost of World War II was about $460 billion. The estimated cost of bailing out the S&Ls will be at least $500 billion. So, as *The Wall Street Journal* recently noted, the S&L bailout will cost $40 billion more than World War II. As for the state of the banks…well, it would appear that we have been robbed.

It is a commonplace that half of those qualified to vote for President don't vote; also, that half the adult population never read a newspaper. No bad thing, all in all, assuming that they *could* read a newspaper, which is moot as our public schools are among the worst in the First World while our prison population, is now the highest, surpassing at last South Africa and the *ci-devant* Soviet Union. Naturally, we lead the First World in the execution of criminals or "criminals."

Every four years the naive half who vote are encouraged to believe that if we can elect a really nice man or woman President everything will be all right. But it won't be. Any individual who is able to raise $25 million to be considered presidential is not going to be much use to the people at large. He will represent oil, or aerospace, or banking, or whatever moneyed entities are paying for him. Certainly he will never represent the people of the country, and they know it. Hence, the sense of despair throughout the land as incomes fall, businesses fail and there is no redress.

Before the national security state was invented, we had something called "representative government." It did not work awfully well but a least there was a sense that, from time to time, something might be done about a depression—the sort of thing that cannot be done by a system in which most public revenues are earmarked for weaponry and war and secret police forces and, of course, the servicing of trillions of dollars' worth of debt.

"When we suffer, or are exposed to the same miseries *by a government,* which we might expect in a country *without government,* our calamities is [sic] heightened by reflecting that we furnish the means by which we suffer. Government, like dress, is the badge of lost innocence; the palaces of kings are built on the ruins of the bowers of paradise." I quote from *Common Sense,* by Thomas Paine.

How do we get rid of this bad government? There is certainly no road back to Eden in any society. Even if we could return, our own Eden was a most serpentine affair, based as it was on the enslavement of Africans and the slaughter and deportation of an indigenous population.

But until 1950, when our ramshackle world empire was institutionalized as the national security state, we *were* improving ourselves, and the generality took part in government while Opinion was not so cynically and totally manipulated as now. Since we cannot pay for the empire any longer, we shall soon be coming home—but to what?

Our "inalienable" rights are being systematically alienated. Never has an American government been so busy interfering with the private lives of its citizens, subjecting them to mandatory blood, urine, lie-detector tests. Yet the war on drugs has nothing at all to do with drugs. It is part of an all-out war on the American people by a government interested only in control.

As this grows more evident, I suspect that we shall begin to see an organized resistance to so tyrannous a state. Meanwhile, as we have neither political parties nor, indeed, politics, only issueless elections, I see only one peaceful way out of this corpse of a Republic, this literally bankrupt national security state.

Article Five of the Constitution describes two methods whereby it may be amended or otherwise altered. One way, and so far the only way yet taken, is by a vote of two-thirds of both houses of Congress. The amendment is then sent for ratification by the state legislatures. The *second* procedure is very interesting indeed—in fact, one might almost call it democratic.

Two-thirds of the state legislatures can request a constitutional convention, which Congress must then convene. Unlike us, the founders did not worship their handiwork. Many thought the original Constitution was bound to fail. Thomas Jefferson wanted to hold a constitutional convention at least once a generation because, as he said, you cannot expect a man to wear a boy's jacket. As it turned out, the jacket has been so reshaped over the past two centuries that it is now a straitjacket for the people at large and satisfying to no one except those who gain election— and profits—from a most peculiar institution.

In recent years there have been several movements to convene a constitutional convention. These efforts have been the work of single-interest groups, usually on the far right. One group wants to forbid abortion to every woman. Another wants a balanced budget embedded in the Constitution. What *is* interesting is that in the 1970s and 1980s thirty-two state legislatures voted in favor of such a convention; but many of them cautiously noted that no subject other than a balanced budget, say, could be discussed.

In 1967 Senator Sam Ervin was so intrigued by Article Five that he thoroughly researched the subject and explained the mechanics of such a convention in S.2307. He came to the conclusion that, as *We the People* are the true de jure sovereign of these states, *We the People* cannot be held by anyone to any single issue once *we* convene *our* convention. If we so choose, the entire Constitution could be rewritten.

At this point I part company with the American Civil Liberties Union, who, for once, are more pessimistic about the people than I. The first thing *they* will get rid of is the Bill of Rights, the liberals moan. To which the answer is, first, I don't think the people are suicidal and, second, what is the difference between losing those rights at an open convention as opposed to a gradual loss of them behind the closed doors of the current Supreme Court?

It is true that we are a less homogeneous and less educated people than the 3 million original inhabitants of the thirteen colonies. But I cannot believe that our convention would do away with our liberties while granting more power, say, to the Executive to fight wars that in the end harm only *us*.

I am aware that the people at large have been kept ignorant by bad schools and by the dispensers of false Opinion. That is true. That is a problem. But ignorance is not stupidity. And self-interest, as both Hamilton and Madison agreed, is a great motor to the state, properly checked and balanced.

In any case, we are now faced with the fury of those who have been deprived for too long of decent lives. It takes no unusual power of prophecy to remark that they will not be apathetic forever. "If it be not now, yet it will come. The readiness is all." Rather than be *un*ready for anarchy, I submit that we must sit down and in an orderly way rethink our entire government as well as our place in the world.

The founders' last gift to us is the machinery to set things right. Article Five. Let us use it.

Thus, I ended my speech to the National Press Club—outrageously, of course.

The Nation
January 27, 1992
*(based in part on a speech given at the
National Press Club)*

Should Our Intelligence Services Be Abolished?

Article 1, Section 9 of the Constitution requires government agencies to submit their budgets at regular intervals to Congress for review. Neither the CIA nor the DIA* does this. Occasionally, at the dark of the moon, they will send someone up to the Hill to mis- and disinform Congress, and that's that. After all, to explain what they actually do with the money that they get would be a breach of national security, the overall rubric that protects so many of them from criminal indictments.

Although most Americans now think that the CIA was created at Valley Forge by General Washington, this unaccountable spy service was invented less than half a century ago, and since that time we have been systematically misinformed about the rest of the world for domestic policy reasons (remember Russia's outstanding economic surge in the 1970s?). Intelligence is an empty concept unless directly related to action. In a war, knowledge of the enemy's troop movements is all-important. In peacetime, random intelligence gathering is meaningless, when not sinister.

---

* [The Defense Intelligence Agency (DIA) is the Defense Department's counterpart to the CIA.]

Since our rulers have figured that one out, they have done their best to make sure that we shall never be at peace; hence, the necessity of tracking enemies—mostly imaginary ones, as the Pentagon recently revealed in its wonderfully wild scenarios for future wars. Since Communism's ultimate crime against humanity was to go out of business, we now have no universal war to conduct except the one against drugs (more than $20 billion was wasted in 1991 on this crusade).

As there is now no longer sufficient money for any of these "wars," there is no longer a rationale for so many secret services unless the Feds really come out of the closet and declare war on the American people, the ultimate solution: After all, one contingency plan in Ollie North's notebook suggested that in a time of crisis, dusky-hued Americans should be sequestered.

I would suggest that the State Department return to its once-useful if dull task of supplying us with information about other countries, so that we might know more about what they'd like to buy from us. The hysterical tracking down of nuclear weapons is useless. After all, we, or our treasured allies, have armed all the world to the teeth.

We have neither the money nor the brains to monitor every country on earth, which means, alas, that if some evil dictator in Madagascar wants to nuke or biologically degrade Washington, D.C., there's not much we can do about it. Certainly, the CIA, as now constituted, would be the last to know of his intention, though perhaps the first to get the good of his foul plot.

I would abandon all the military-related secret services and I would keep the F.B.I. on a tight leash—no more dirty tricks against those who dislike the way that we are governed, and no more dossiers on those of us who might be able to find a way out of the mess we are in, best personified by the late J. Edgar Hoover and best memorialized by that Pennsylvania Avenue Babylonian fortress that still bears his infamous name.

The Nation
June 8, 1992

Monotheism and Its Discontents

It is very easy to discuss *what* has gone wrong with us. It is not so easy to discuss what should be done to correct what has gone wrong. It is absolutely impossible in our public discourse to discuss *why* so much has gone wrong and, indeed, has been wrong with us since the very beginning of the country, and even before that when our white tribes were living elsewhere.

Unfortunately, there are two subjects that we are never permitted to discuss with any seriousness: race and religion, and how our attitudes toward the first are rooted in the second. Thanks to this sternly—correctly?—enforced taboo, we are never able to get to the root of our problems. We are like people born in a cage and unable to visualize any world beyond our familiar bars of prejudice and superstition. That Opinion the Few create in order to control the Many* has seen to it that we are kept in permanent ignorance of our actual estate.

Even so, a number of prisoners are testing the bars. Some actually got loose in Los Angeles, for a weekend. The wardens are alarmed.

---

* [See the quote from David Hume on p. 40.]

The two trustees they are offering us are not acceptable to the restive prison population, while, out of Texas, strode a small but imperfectly formed man, differently, gloriously advantaged sizewise, and in his tiny paw, there was—no, it can't be but yes, it did look very like—a *key*. Oh, Ross, free at last! Failing that, build us a better, more prisoner-friendly cage. But Ross went home, taking his key with him.

A political analyst wrote at the time of the New Hampshire primary that the two irrelevant candidates for President this year, Jerry Brown and Pat Buchanan, should leave the field to the heavyweights—like Bush and Clinton. As the media are a large part of the mess that we are in, the journalist—deliberately?—got it wrong.

Brown and Buchanan were the only substantive, relevant and representative—in the best and worst senses—candidates on display. So let us brood on them and what it is that they represent in the way of race and religion, the two root issues.

The word "radical" derives from the Latin word for root. Therefore, if you want to get to the root of *any*thing you must be radical. It is no accident that the word has now been totally demonized by our masters, and no one in politics dares even to use the word favorably, much less track any problem to its root.

But then a ruling class that was able to demonize the word "liberal" in the past ten years is a master at controlling—indeed stifling—any criticism of itself.

"Liberal" comes from the Latin *liberalis,* which means pertaining to a free man. In politics, to be liberal is to want to extend democracy through change and reform. One can see why that word had to be erased from our political lexicon.

Meanwhile, the word "isolationist" has been revised to describe those who would like to put an end to the national security state that replaced our Republic a half-century ago, while extending the American military empire far beyond our capacity to pay for it. The word was trotted out this year to describe Pat Buchanan, when he was causing great distress to the managers of our national security state by saying that America must abandon the empire if we are ever to repair the mess at home.

Also, as a neo-isolationist, Buchanan must be made to seem an anti-Semite. This is not hard to do. Buchanan is a classic Archie Bunker type, seething with irrational prejudices and resentments, whose origin I will get to presently.

The country is now dividing, as it did a half-century ago, between those who think that

America comes first versus those who favor empire and the continued exertion of force everywhere in the name of democracy, something not much on display here at home. In any case, as the whole world is, more or less, a single economic unit in which the United States is an ever smaller component, there are no isolationists today.

But the word games go on and the deliberate reversals of meaning are always a sign that our corporate masters are worried that the people are beginning to question their arrangements. Many things are now coming into focus. *The New York Times* promptly dismissed Buchanan as a minor irritant, which was true, but it ignored his potentially major constituency—those who now believe that it was a mistake to have wasted, since 1950, most of the government's revenues on war.

Jerry Brown alarmed the *Times* even more than Buchanan did. There was the possibility that he could be elected. More important, he might actually change our politics in the sense of who pays for whom.

In a sudden frenzy, the *Times* compared him to Perón—our Jerry?—a dangerous demagogue whose "sharp-edged anger...resonates among a variety of Americans." Plainly, the ownership of the country is frightened that the current hatred of politicians, in general, may soon be translated into a hatred of that corporate few who control the many through Opinion, as manufactured by the *Times*, among others.

Now to the root of the matter. The great unmentionable evil at the center of our culture is monotheism. From a barbaric Bronze Age text known as the Old Testament, three antihuman religions have evolved—Judaism, Christianity and Islam. These are sky-god religions. They are, literally, patriarchal— God is the omnipotent father—hence the loathing of women for 2,000 years in those countries afflicted by the sky-god and his earthly male delegates.

The sky-god is a jealous god, of course. He requires total obedience from everyone on earth, as he is in place not just for one tribe but all creation. Those who would reject him must be converted or killed for their own good.

Ultimately, totalitarianism is the only sort of politics that can truly serve the sky-god's purpose. Any movement of a liberal nature endangers his authority and that of his delegates on earth. One God, one King, one Pope, one master in the factory, one father-leader in the family at home.

The founders of the United States were not enthusiasts of the sky-god. Many, like Jefferson, rejected him altogether and placed man at the center of the world. The young Lincoln wrote a pamphlet *against* Christianity, which friends persuaded him to burn. Needless to say, word got around about both Jefferson and Lincoln and each had to cover his tracks. Jefferson said that he was a deist, which could mean anything or nothing, while Lincoln, hand on heart and tongue in cheek, said he could not support for office anyone who "scoffed" at religion.

From the beginning, sky-godders have always exerted great pressure in our secular republic. Also, evangelical Christian groups have traditionally drawn strength from the suppressed. African slaves were allowed to organize heavenly sky-god churches, as a surrogate for earthly freedom. White churches were organized in order to make certain that the rights of property were respected and that the numerous religious taboos in the New and Old Testaments would be enforced, if necessary, by civil law.

The ideal to which John Adams subscribed— that we would be a nation of laws, not of men—was quickly subverted when the churches forced upon everyone, through supposedly neutral and just laws, their innumerable taboos on sex, alcohol, gambling. We are now indeed a nation of laws, mostly bad and certainly antihuman.

Roman Catholic migrations in the last century further reinforced the Puritan sky-god. The Church has also put itself on a collision course with the Bill of Rights when it asserts, as it always has, that "error has no rights." The last correspondence between John Adams and Thomas Jefferson expressed their alarm that the Jesuits were to be allowed into the United States.

Although the Jews were sky-god folk, they followed Book One, not Book Two, so they have no mission to convert others; rather the reverse. Also, as they have been systematically demonized by the Christian sky-godders, they tended to be liberal and so turned not to their temple but to the ACLU. Unfortunately, the recent discovery that the sky-god, in his capacity as realtor, had given them, in perpetuity, some parcels of unattractive land called Judea and Samaria has, to my mind, unhinged many of them. I hope this is temporary.

In the First Amendment to the Constitution, the Founders made it clear that this was not to be a sky-god nation with a national religion like that of England, from whom we had just separated. It is curious how little understood this amendment is—yes, everyone has a right to worship any god he chooses but he does *not* have the right to impose his beliefs on others who do not happen to share in his superstitions and taboos.

This separation was absolute in our original Republic. But the sky-godders do not give up easily. In the 1950s they actually got the phrase "In God We Trust" onto the currency, in direct violation of the First Amendment.

Although many of the Christian evangelists feel it necessary to convert everyone on earth to their primitive religion, they have been prevented—so far—from forcing others to worship as they do, but they *have* forced—most tyrannically and wickedly—their superstitions and hatreds upon all of us through the civil law and through general prohibitions. So it is upon that account that I now favor an all-out war on the monotheists.

Let us dwell upon the evils they have wrought. The hatred of blacks comes straight from their Bad Book. As descendants of Ham, blacks are forever accursed, while Saint Paul tells the slaves to obey their masters. Racism is in the marrow of the bone of the true believer. For him, black is forever inferior to white and deserves whatever ill fortune may come his way.

The fact that some monotheists can behave charitably means, often, that their prejudice is at so deep a level that they are not aware it is there at all. In the end, this makes any radical change of attitude impossible. Meanwhile, welfare has been the price the sky-godders were willing to pay to exclude blacks from their earthly political system. So we must live—presumably forever—with a highly enervating race war, set in train by the One God and his many hatreds.

Patriarchal rage at the thought of Woman ever usurping Man's place at the helm, in either home or workplace, is almost as strong now as it ever was. According to the polls at the time of the hearings, most American women took the side of Clarence Thomas against Anita Hill. But then the sky-god's fulminations against women are still very much part of the psyche of those in thrall to the Jealous God.

The ongoing psychopathic hatred of same-sexuality has made the United States the laughingstock of the civilized world. In most of the First World, monotheism is weak. Where it is weak or nonexistent, private sexual behavior has nothing at all to do with those not involved, much less with the law.

At least when the Emperor Justinian, a sky-god man, decided to outlaw sodomy, he had to come up with a good *practical* reason, which he did. It is well known, Justinian declared, that buggery is a principal cause of earthquakes, and so must be prohibited. But our sky-godders, always eager to hate, still quote Leviticus, as if that loony text had anything useful to say about anything except, perhaps, the inadvisability of eating shellfish in the Jerusalem area.

We are now, slowly, becoming alarmed at the state of the planet. For a century, we have been breeding like a virus under optimum conditions, and now the virus has begun to attack its host, the earth. The lower atmosphere is filled with dust, we have just been told from our satellites in space. Climate changes; earth and water are poisoned. Sensible people grow alarmed, but sky-godders are serene, even smug. The planet is just a staging area for heaven. Why bother to clean it up?

Unfortunately for everyone, George Bush's only hope of winning in the coming election is to appeal to the superstitious. So at Rio he refused to commit our government to the great cleanup, partly because it would affect the incomes of the 100 corporate men and women who pay for him, but largely because of the sky-god, who told his slaves to "be fruitful and multiply, and replenish the earth, and subdue it, and have dominion...over every living thing that moveth upon the earth." Well, we did just like you told us, massa. We've used everything up. We're ready for heaven now. Or maybe Mars will do.

Ordinarily, as a descendant of the eighteenth-century Enlightenment, which shaped our Republic, I would say live and let live and I would try not to "scoff"—to use Lincoln's verb—at the monotheists. But I am not allowed to ignore them. They won't let me. They are too busy. They have a divine mission to take away our rights as private citizens.

We are forbidden abortion here, gambling there, same-sex almost everywhere, drugs, alcohol in a dry county. Our prisons are the most terrible and the most crowded in the First World. Our death row executions are a source of deep disgust in civilized countries, where more and more we are regarded as a primitive, uneducated and dangerous people. Although we are not allowed, under law, to kill ourselves or to take drugs that the good folk think might be bad for us, we are allowed to buy a handgun and shoot as many people as we can get away with.

Of course, as poor Arthur (There Is This Pendulum) Schlesinger Jr. would say, these things come in cycles. Every twenty years liberal gives way to conservative, and back again. But I suggest that what is wrong now is not cyclic but systemic. And our system, like any system, is obeying the second law of thermodynamics. Everything is running down; and we are well advanced along the yellow brick road to entropy.

I don't think much of anything can be done to halt this progress under our present political-economic system. We lost poor Arthur's pendulum in 1950 when our original Constitution was secretly replaced with the apparatus of the national security state, which still wastes most of our tax money on war or war-related matters. Hence deteriorating schools, and so on.

Another of our agreed-upon fantasies is that we do not have a class system in the United States. The Few who control the Many through Opinion have simply made themselves invisible. They have convinced us that we are a classless society in which anyone can make it.

Ninety percent of the stories in the pop press are about winners of lotteries or poor boys and girls who, despite adenoidal complaints, become overnight millionaire singers. So there is still hope, the press tells the folks, for the 99 percent who will never achieve wealth no matter how hard they work. We are also warned at birth that it is not polite to hurt people's feelings by criticizing their religion, even if that religion may be damaging everyone through the infiltration of our common laws.

Happily, the few cannot disguise the bad times through which we are all going. Word is spreading that America is now falling behind in the civilization sweepstakes. So isn't it time to discuss what we all really think and feel about our social and economic arrangements?

Although we may not discuss race other than to say that Jesus wants each and every one of us for a sunbeam, history is nothing more than the bloody record of the migration of tribes. When the white race broke out of Europe 500 years ago, it did many astounding things all over the globe. Inspired by a raging sky-god, the whites were able to pretend that their conquests were in order to bring the One God to everyone, particularly those with older and subtler religions.

Now the tribes are on the move again. Professor Pendulum is having a nervous breakdown because so many different tribes are now being drawn to this sweet land of liberty and, thus far, there is no indication that any of the new arrivals intends ever to read *The Age of Jackson*. I think the taking in of everyone can probably be overdone. There may not be enough jobs for very many more immigrants, though what prosperity we have ever enjoyed in the past was usually based on slave or near-slave labor.

On the other hand, I think Asians, say, are a plus culturally, and their presence tends to refocus, somewhat, the relentless white versus black war. Where I *am* as one with friend Pendulum is that the newcomers must grasp certain principles as expressed in the Declaration of Independence and the Bill of Rights. Otherwise, we shall become a racially divided totalitarian state enjoying a Brazilian economy.

To revert to the unmentionable, religion. It should be noted that religion seemed to be losing its hold in the United States in the second quarter of this century. From the Scopes trial in '25 to the repeal of Prohibition in '33, the sky-godders were confined pretty much to the backwoods. Then television was invented and the electronic pulpit was soon occupied by a horde of Elmer Gantrys, who took advantage of the tax exemption for religion. Thus, out of greed, a religious revival has been set in motion and the results are predictably poisonous to the body politic.

It is usual, on the rare occasions when essential problems are addressed, to exhort everyone to be kinder, gentler. To bring us together, O Lord, in our common humanity. Well, we have heard these exhortations for a couple of hundred years and we are further apart than ever.

So instead of coming together in order that the many might be one, I say let us separate so that each will know where he stands. From the *one, many,* and each of us free of the sky-god as secular lawgiver. I preach, to put it bluntly, confrontation.

Brown and Buchanan, whether they knew it or not, were revealing two basic, opposing political movements. Buchanan speaks for the party of God—the sky-god with his terrible hatred of women, blacks, gays, drugs, abortion, contraception, gambling—you name it, he hates it.

Buchanan is a worthy peddler of hate. He is also in harmony not only with the prejudices and superstitions of a good part of the population but, to give him his due, he is a reactionary in the good sense—reacting against the empire in favor of the old Republic, which he mistakenly thinks was Christian.

Brown speaks for the party of man—feminists can find another noun if they like. Thomas Paine, when asked *his* religion, said he subscribed only to the religion of humanity.

There now seems to be a polarizing of the country of a sort that has never happened before. The potential fault line has always been there, but whenever a politician got too close to the facts of our case, the famed genius of the system would eliminate him in favor of that mean which is truly golden for the ownership, and no one else.

The party of man would like to re-establish a representative government firmly based upon the Bill of Rights. The party of God will have none of this. It wants to establish, through legal prohibitions and enforced taboos, a sky-god totalitarian state. The United States ultimately as prison, with mandatory blood, urine and lie-detector tests and with the sky-godders as the cops, answerable only to God, who sent us and then, mysteriously, took back his Only Son, H. Ross Perot, as warden.

For once, it's all out there, perfectly visible, perfectly plain for those who can see. That Brown and Buchanan will not figure in the election does not alter the fact that, for the first time in 140 years, we now have, due in part to their efforts, the outline of two parties. Each knows the nature of its opposite, and those who are wise will not try to accommodate or compromise the two but will let them, at last, confront each other.

The famous tree of liberty is all that we have ever really had. Now, for want of nurture, it is dying before our eyes. Of course, the sky-god never liked it. But some of us did—and some of us do. So, perhaps, through facing who and what we are, we may achieve a nation not under God but under man—or should I say our common humanity?

The Nation
July 13, 1992
(adapted from the 1992 Lowell Lecture
at Harvard)

Recommended Reading

Bagdikian, Ben. *The Media Monopoly,* third revised edition. Beacon Press, 1990.

Chomsky, Noam. *What Uncle Sam Really Wants.* Odonian Press, 1992.

Domhoff, G. William. *Who Rules America Now?* Prentice Hall, 1983. Touchstone, 1986.

— *The Power Elite and the State: How Policy is Made in America.* Aldine de Gruyter (200 Saw Mill River Road, Hawthorne, NY 10532; 914 747 0110), 1990.

Halsell, Grace. *Prophecy and Politics: Militant Evangelists on the Road to Nuclear War.* Lawrence Hill and Co (230 Park Place, Suite 6A, Brooklyn NY 11238; 800 888 4741), 1986.

Herman, Edward S. and Noam Chomsky. *Manufacturing Consent: the Political Economy of the Mass Media.* Pantheon Books, 1988.

The Nation. Published weekly (except for the first week in January and biweekly in July and August). Subscription information: Box 10763, Des Moines IA 50340; 800 333 8536. (There are also order forms in each copy.)

Shapiro, H. R. *Democracy in America.* Manhattan Communications (513 Wilshire Blvd, #220, Santa Monica CA 90401), 1990.

Books by Gore Vidal

Novels

Williwaw • *In a Yellow Wood*
The City and the Pillar • *The Season of Comfort*
A Search for the King • *Dark Green, Bright Red*
The Judgment of Paris • *Messiah* • *Julian*
Washington, D.C. • *Myra Breckinridge*
Two Sisters • *Burr* • *Myron* • *1876*
Kalki • *Creation* • *Duluth* • *Lincoln*
Empire • *Hollywood* • *Live from Golgotha*

Essays

Rocking the Boat
Reflections upon a Sinking Ship
Homage to Daniel Shays
Matters of Fact and Fiction
The Second American Revolution
At Home • *Screening History*
The Decline and Fall of the American Empire

Plays

An Evening with Richard Nixon
Weekend • *Romulus*
The Best Man • *Visit to a Small Planet*

Short stories

A Thirsty Evil

Interviews

Views from a Window

Index

*The Real Story series
is based on a simple idea—
political books don't have to be boring.
Short, well-written and to the point,
Real Story books are meant to be <u>read</u>.*

*If you liked this book,
check out some of the others:*

What Uncle Sam Really Wants
Noam Chomsky
A brilliant analysis of the real motivations behind US foreign policy, from one of America's most popular speakers. Full of astounding information.   *Fall, 1992*

Burma: The Next Killing Fields?
Alan Clements
If we don't do something about Burma, it will become another Cambodia. Written by one of the few Westerners ever to have lived there, this book tells the story vividly.   *Summer, 1992*

Who Killed JFK?   Carl Oglesby
This brief but fact-filled book gives you the inside story on the most famous crime of this century. You won't be able to put it down.   *Spring, 1992*